Butterflies

Debbie and Brendan Gallagher

Marshall Cavendish
Benchmark

New York

This edition first published in 2012 in the United States of America by Marshall Cavendish Benchmark
An imprint of Marshall Cavendish Corporation

Website: www.marshallcavendish.us

This publication represents the opinions and views of the authors based on Debbie and Brendan Gallagher's personal experiences, knowledge, and research. The information in this book serves as a general guide only. The authors and publisher have used their best efforts in preparing this book and disclaim liability rising directly and indirectly from the use and application of this book.

Other Marshall Cavendish Offices:
Marshall Cavendish Ltd. 5th Floor, 32-38 Saffron Hill, London EC1N 8 FH, UK • Marshall Cavendish International (Asia) Private Limited, 1 New Industrial Road, Singapore 536196 • Marshall Cavendish International (Thailand) Co Ltd. 253 Asoke, 12th Flr, Sukhumvit 21 Road, Klongtoey Nua, Wattana, Bangkok 10110, Thailand • Marshall Cavendish (Malaysia) Sdn Bhd, Times Subang, Lot 46, Subang Hi-Tech Industrial Park, Batu Tiga, 40000 Shah Alam, Selangor Darul Ehsan, Malaysia

Marshall Cavendish is a trademark of Times Publishing Limited

All websites were available and accurate when this book was sent to press.

Library of Congress Cataloging-in-Publication Data

Gallagher, Debbie, 1969–
  Butterflies / Debbie Gallagher.
    p. cm. — (Mighty minibeasts)
  Includes index.
  Summary: "Discusses the features, habitat, food, life cycle, living habits, and unique behaviors of butterflies"—Provided by publisher.
  ISBN 978-1-60870-544-3
  1. Butterflies—Juvenile literature. I. Title.
  QL544.2 .G343 2012
  595.78/9—dc22
                                2010037193

First published in 2011 by
MACMILLAN EDUCATION AUSTRALIA PTY LTD
15–19 Claremont Street, South Yarra 3141

Visit our website at www.macmillan.com.au or go directly to www.macmillanlibrary.com.au

Associated companies and representatives throughout the world.

Copyright Text © Debbie Gallagher 2011

Publisher: Carmel Heron
Commissioning Editor: Niki Horin
Managing Editor: Vanessa Lanaway
Editor: Tim Clarke
Proofreader: Gill Owens
Designer: Kerri Wilson (cover and text)
Page layout: Domenic Lauricella
Photo research: Legendimages
Illustrator: Gaston Vanzet
Production Controller: Vanessa Johnson

Printed in China

Acknowledgments
The authors and the publisher are grateful to the following for permission to reproduce copyright material:

Front cover photograph: A dark green fritillary butterfly © Photolibrary/Otto Hahn.
Photographs courtesy of: Auscape/Densey Clyne, **28**; Dreamstime.com/Neil Harrison, **10** (bottom); Getty Images/ Lori Adamski Peek, **30**, /Richard Ellis, **22**, /Mattias Klum, **19**, / Panoramic Images, **12**; iStockphoto/ParkerDeen, **14** (top); naturepl.com/Nick Upton, **13**; Photolibrary/Scott Camazine, **24**, /Er. Degginger, **9** (bottom), /Philip J DeVries, **29**, /Reinhard Dirscherl, **6**, /Michael Fogden, **21** (bottom), /Otto Hahn, **1**, **27**, / Joël Héras, **9** (top), /Nature's Images, **21** (center above), /OSF/ London Scientific Films, **20**, /Barbara Strnadova, **8** (bottom), / Philip Tull, **17**, /James Urbach, **7**; Shutterstock/Anson0618, **5**, **21** (top), /Ariel Bravy, **16**, /goran cakmazovic, **21** (center below), /Dewayne Flowers, **25**, /Trish Gaunt, **11** (bottom left), /Ivan Hor, **4**, /Cathy Keifer, **14** (bottom), **15** (both), /Tomas Pavelka, **11** (bottom right), /Dr Morley Read, **18**, /Sue Robinson, **3**, **11** (top left), /Ashley Whitworth, **11** (bottom center); Wikimedia Commons/Kenneth Dwain Harrelson, **10** (top), /Laitche, **11** (top right), /Mark Pellegrini, **8** (top).

While every care has been taken to trace and acknowledge copyright, the publisher tenders their apologies for any accidental infringement where copyright has proved untraceable. They would be pleased to come to a suitable arrangement with the rightful owner in each case.

1 3 5 6 4 2

Contents

When a word is printed in **bold**, you can look up its meaning in the Glossary on page 31.

Mighty Minibeasts

Minibeasts are small animals, such as flies and spiders. Although they are small, minibeasts are a mighty collection of animals. They belong to three animal groups: arthropods, molluscs, or annelids.

	Animal Group		
	Arthropods	**Molluscs**	**Annelids**
Main Feature	Arthropods have an outer skeleton and a body that is divided into sections.	Most molluscs have a soft body that is not divided into sections.	Annelids have a soft body made up of many sections.
Examples of Minibeasts	Insects, such as ants, beetles, cockroaches, and wasps **Arachnids**, such as spiders and scorpions Centipedes and millipedes	Snails and slugs	Earthworms Leeches

More than three-quarters of all animals are minibeasts!

Butterflies

Butterflies are minibeasts. They belong to the arthropod group of animals. This means they have an outer skeleton and a body that is divided into sections. Butterflies are a type of insect.

Butterflies are closely related to moths.

What Do Butterflies Look Like?

Butterflies have a narrow body divided into three main parts. These parts are the head, the **thorax**, and the **abdomen**. Butterflies have four wings and six legs.

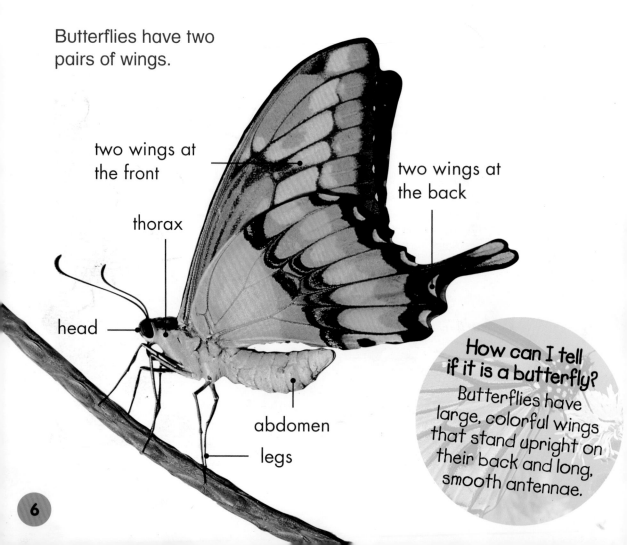

Butterflies have two pairs of wings.

two wings at the front

two wings at the back

thorax

head

abdomen

legs

How can I tell if it is a butterfly? Butterflies have large, colorful wings that stand upright on their back and long, smooth antennae.

Butterflies have scales on their wings and tiny hairs covering their body. They have long **antennae** attached to their head. Their mouth is called a **proboscis**.

Butterflies use their special features to sense the world around them.

antennae for smelling

proboscis for eating

scales for sensing sounds

hairs for feeling

Different Types of Butterflies

There are more than 13,500 different **species** of butterflies. The largest butterflies are 12 inches (30 centimeters) from wingtip to wingtip. The smallest butterflies are ¼ inch (6 millimeters) from wingtip to wingtip.

Birdwings are the largest butterflies.

12 inches (30 centimeters)

The pygmy blue is one of the smallest species of butterflies.

¼ inch (6 millimeters)

Some butterflies have colors or patterns on their wings. This helps them to hide from or scare away **predators**.

Some butterflies have wings that look like leaves, which helps them to hide among plants.

Owl butterflies have wings that look like owl eyes, to scare away predators.

Where in the World Are Butterflies Found?

Butterflies can be found on every continent except Antarctica. They can also be found on most islands.

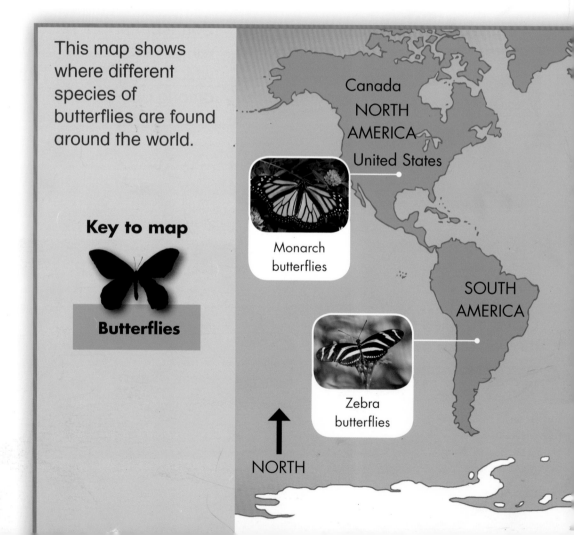

This map shows where different species of butterflies are found around the world.

Key to map

Butterflies

Canada

NORTH AMERICA

United States

Monarch butterflies

SOUTH AMERICA

Zebra butterflies

NORTH

Butterflies are not found in places where it is too dry or too cold.

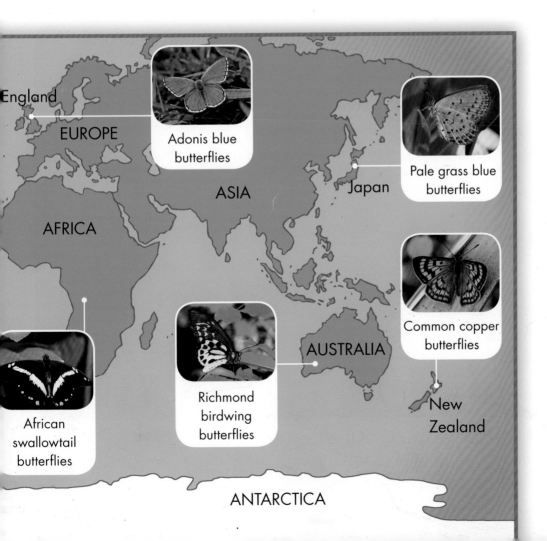

England

EUROPE

Adonis blue butterflies

ASIA

Japan

Pale grass blue butterflies

AFRICA

Common copper butterflies

AUSTRALIA

African swallowtail butterflies

Richmond birdwing butterflies

New Zealand

ANTARCTICA

Habitats of Butterflies

Butterflies live in all types of **habitats**. They live in forests, at beaches, and in many deserts. Rain forest habitats have the most species of butterflies.

Rain forests have plenty of the food and shelter that blue morpho butterflies need to live.

Butterflies can also live in cold habitats, such as high up on mountains, if there is food and shelter. If it gets too cold, butterflies move somewhere warmer.

In cold places, butterflies rest on rocks that have become warm in the sun.

Life Cycles of Butterflies

A life cycle diagram shows the stages of a butterfly's life, from newborn to adult.

1. A male and a female butterfly **mate**. The female lays eggs on a plant that will be good food for the young.

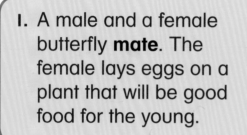

egg

4. A butterfly comes out of the chrysalis after one or two weeks. Once its wings are dry it can fly away.

Most butterflies live for only a few weeks or months. In this time they must mate and lay eggs that will hatch new caterpillars.

2. A caterpillar hatches from each egg and eats until it has grown to full size. As it grows, the caterpillar changes its skin several times. This is called molting.

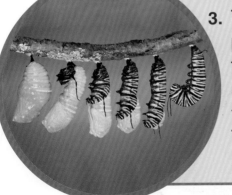

3. The fully grown caterpillar is called a **pupa** (say *pyoo-pa*). The pupa's skin forms a hard casing called a chrysalis (say *kriss-a-liss*). Inside the chrysalis, the pupa changes into a butterfly. This is called metamorphosis (say *met-a-more-fa-siss*).

How Do Butterflies Live?

Most butterflies are active during the day. They use their wings to sense danger by feeling changes in sound. They use their antennae to smell and their feet to taste.

Butterflies use special pads on their feet to taste their food.

feet with pads

Butterflies often rest in sunny spots. This is because butterflies are cold-blooded. This means their body will be hot or cold depending on the temperature around them.

A butterfly can warm its body by resting in the sun.

Butterfly Homes

Butterflies do not live in homes such as nests. Instead, they make a whole area their home. When they need to rest or take shelter, they hide under leaves or rocks.

Butterflies can hang upside down from leaves when they need to rest.

A butterfly's home area may be small if there is plenty of food. When there is less food, a butterfly will have a large home area.

Where there is lots of food, many butterflies can share the same home area.

Butterfly Food

Butterflies can only eat liquid foods. They use their proboscis to suck up **nectar** from many different types of flowers.

A butterfly uses its proboscis like a straw to drink its food.

proboscis

Butterflies drink the sweet liquid made by trees, called sap. They also drink the liquid from rotting fruit, mud, animal droppings, and even dead animals.

Foods That Butterflies Eat

Flower nectar

Muddy water

Fruit juice

Tree sap

Why Do Butterflies Migrate?

Some butterflies migrate, or move from one area to another, to escape cold weather. In winter they move to a warmer area.

Monarch butterflies gather into large groups to migrate together.

Some monarch butterflies migrate thousands of miles. In summer they live in the northern United States. In winter they travel south to Mexico, where it is warmer.

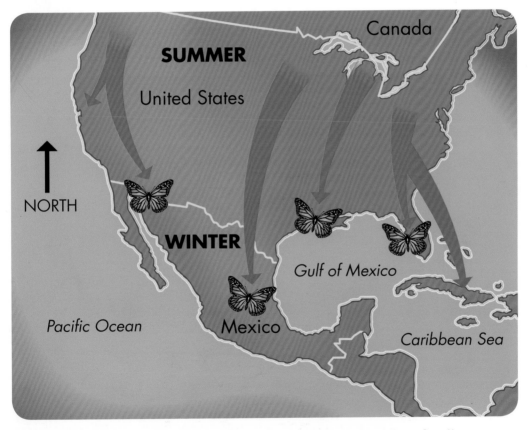

In winter, monarch butterflies migrate thousands of miles across the United States to warmer places.

Threats to the Survival of Butterflies

Butterflies are threatened by other animals. Many different predators eat butterflies and their young. These predators include ants, wasps, spiders, birds, and mice.

A Chinese mantis has caught this butterfly to eat.

Butterflies can only lay their eggs on certain types of plants. The survival of butterflies is threatened when humans remove these plants.

When humans build roads, they sometimes destroy the plants that butterflies need to live.

Butterflies and the Environment

Butterflies are an important part of the **environment** they live in. Butterflies feed on other animals and on plants, and many animals feed on them. This is shown in a food web.

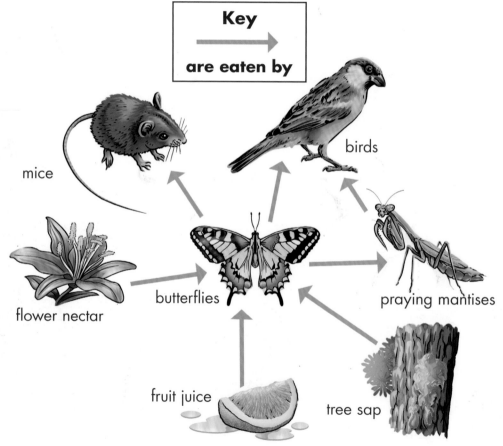

Key
are eaten by

mice

birds

flower nectar

butterflies

praying mantises

fruit juice

tree sap

This food web shows what butterflies eat and what eats them.

Flowers need to spread **pollen** to make new plants. This is called pollination. Butterflies help to pollinate flowers.

This butterfly is picking up pollen on its body as it drinks nectar from a flower.

Butterflies and Ants

Some species of butterflies have a special relationship with ants. These butterflies lay their eggs on plants where ants live. The ants protect the eggs and caterpillars from predators.

Ants chase away any wasps or other predators that come too close to the caterpillar.

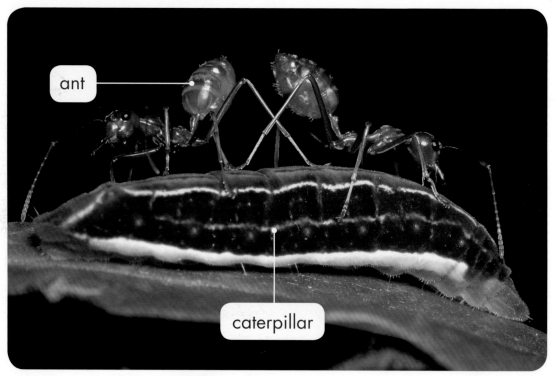

ant

caterpillar

The caterpillars make a sweet milk called honeydew. The ants feed on the honeydew. Both the caterpillars and the ants are helped by their relationship.

These ants are drinking honeydew from the caterpillar.

honeydew

caterpillar

ant

Tips for Watching Butterflies

These tips will help you to watch butterflies:

- Choose a sunny day, when butterflies are more likely to be out in the open.
- Look for butterflies where there are flowers, such as in a garden or a park.
- Move slowly and quietly.
- Remember that your shadow will frighten butterflies.

Look but do not touch! Watch butterflies without touching them to see where they go and what they do.

If you move slowly, you can sometimes get close to a resting butterfly.

Glossary

abdomen   The end section of an insect's body.

antennae   Organs found on the heads of insects, used for sensing things.

arachnids   Eight-legged animals, such as spiders, that are part of the arthropod group.

environment   The air, water, and land that surround us.

habitats   Areas in which animals are naturally found.

mate   Join together to produce young.

nectar   A sweet liquid made by flowers.

pollen   Yellow powder found on flowers.

predators   Animals that hunt other animals for food.

proboscis   A tube used for sucking up food.

pupa   What an insect larva (baby) turns into before becoming an adult.

species   Groups of animals or plants that have similar features.

thorax   The part of the body between the head and abdomen.

Index